where does love go

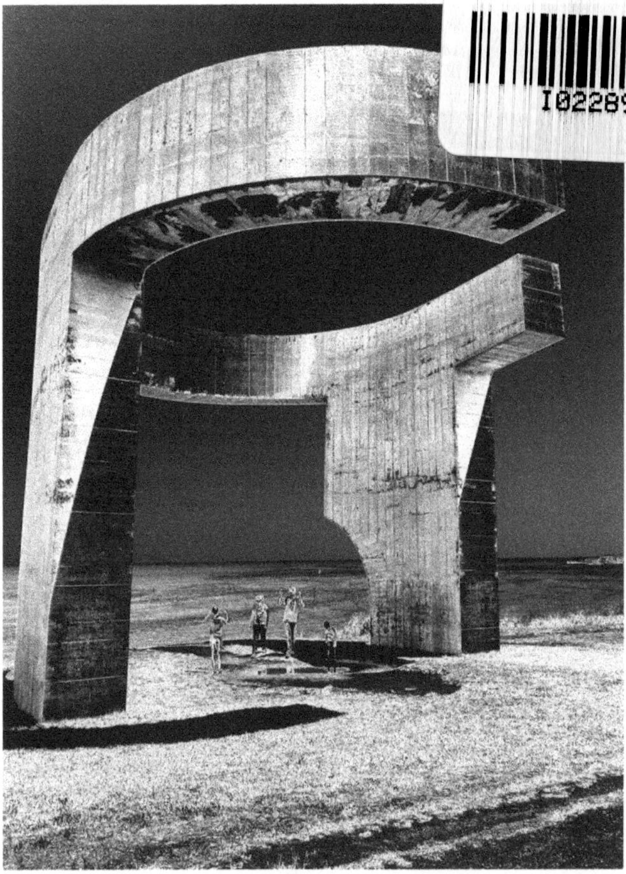

tom murphy

© 2025 Thomas Michael Murphy

All rights reserved. Published 2025

Editor: Christopher Carmona

Interior Design: Isaac Chavarria

Cover Design: Christopher Carmona

Cover Art: Mot

Published By Slough Press

ISBN: 979-8-9993671-0-5

where does love go

Tom Murphy's new book, *where does love go*, is a rip current that will pull your feet out from under you. When you go under, don't panic. Keep reading. Read parallel to the shore of reality until you begin to feel the logic of poetry, then read at an angle until you realize that the windblown Corpus palms you see in the distance, down Ocean Drive, are guiding you to new ways of seeing, of being. Tom Murphy's *where does love go* is the journey of a lifetime, one you'll never forget. Go ahead, read it, take the ride. I dare you. You'll be glad you did.

Ron Whitehead, U.S. National Lifetime Beat Poet Laureate

where does love go is some of Tom Murphy's most engaging poetry to date. This is poetry of mythic energy and forging, foraging the personal and literary landscape seeking context, seeking medicine, seeking the connects held in letting go. The first line of the first poem hangs pregnant in the air throughout, as Murphy reveals, in turn,

>poet as card sharp
>
>poet as worker
>
>poet as traveler

ever arising. Ever crossing lines, crossing borders, crossing convention, Tom Murphy's poetry dancing to the turn it could only call its own.

Rail riding, sparring with Ali, bearing witness to the grave but always making his escape…for now, Tom Murphy has returned from the edge to and he invites us all to join him as he looks up river, as he looks with the eyes of Artemis, as he glides through the French Quarter, as he looks out to sea from his home, when he's home, in Corpus Christi.

PW Covington, NBPF Beat Poet Laureate of New Mexico (2024-2026)

While *where does love go* by Tom Murphy is part travel log, part medical history, part political diatribe, part celebration of love and friendship, part retelling of childhood and adult trauma, part retelling of history and myth, it is in its whole, the baring of the poet's typhus-scarred but healed heart that pulses to its own unique beat. This gift that awaits you just beyond these covers.

Alan Berecka author of *Atlas Sighs: Selected and New Poems*

Tom Murphy's latest poetry volume *where does love go* is a revelation. His new poems speak with a mature tenderness in the face of the exigencies of sudden loss, change and risk. They display an engaging zest for the wanderlust of travel as well as a willingness to unflinchingly explore the intimacies of relationships. Prepare to be challenged, amused and occasionally dazzled as you wander through Tom's unique take on life as we know it now.

Dr. Pamela Brouillard - Clinical Psychologist

The low hanging fruit is the sweetest.

David Wallace PhD, full time dad

As usual, Tom Murphy's poems are zany, witty, full of surprises, begging for multiple readings, unpredictable, no two alike, full of humanity. My kind of poetry. So many good poems. I especially like "7 8 23 Petaluma," "Leap Day Poem," "Lost it all." No accounting for taste. But the one that really captured me is "York Minster." This is a poem of genius. You adapt a line from Jim Morrison's spoken poem, "An American Prayer," but left—sly dog—unreferenced the line central to your poem: "We have assembled inside this ancient and insane theatre to propagate our lust for life." Your prayer mingles at least five theatres: York Minster, pub, St. Jean Baptist Church's celebration of Kerouac in Lowell, music hall, operating room. The sixth theatre is the poem itself ("Fine crenulations"="Fine handwriting"). Different kinds of prayers or offerings are also mingled: organ pieces, stained glass, tavern drinks (Timothy Taylor's Landlord, laughing dog, velvet hour), music (ringtone, muddy waters, Siobhan O'Malley, Led Zeppelin, Jim Morrison, the organist). All this merged with negative prayers (Paypal, orcish, Thrump, Yorkshire Ripper hammers). The horned staff is both a war staff and the medical caduceus. All this amalgamation is absolute: "this poem has no center to reference anymore." "Ubiquitous." How many John Taylors have there been in the history of the world, for good and bad? The poem is a Petri dish. Its significance lies in a hope for the future. So, it's another prayer. A "mess" (= mass) for the future. Pure genius.

Rich Haswell, Haas Professor of English Emeritus, author of *Flora of the Rio Grande Watershed in Colorado*.

In his most recent poetry collection, *where does love go*, Tom Murphy punches the gas pedal of his wild imagination and takes us on a journey that traces the shifting contours of a life redefined by retirement, illness, and, yes, the subtleties of quiet joys. Averse to complacency and stagnation, these poems jump on the interstate, fly across oceans and alight, in the blink of an eye, next to Keats' grave, on a tram in Turkey, or at the edge of the Mississippi. Brimming with grace and gratitude, these poems are Murphy's way to say "thank you" to the places he has been, and to the people in his life, specially to his living poet friends and to those who have gone ahead to clear a path for us to follow their "vast illuminations." Read these poems while your "thirst is still wet," and see how "all is woven."

Octavio Quintanilla— *The Book of Wounded Sparrows* **(Texas Review Press) &** *Las Horas Imposibles / The Impossible Hours* **(University of Arizona Press).**

For Susan

who's always there when I need her most

my love for you

a video of Romeo & Juliet in space

that spins like a satellite

a line straight out of dream

that wakes one from slumber

to be written into poem

before memory fades

into oblivion of the

noisome A/C kicking on

daily your love wakes me, dauntless

forever

And for Alan Berecka

for when I was desperate

And for PW Covington

fellow road dog

And to my poet friends

where does love go originated from two events that came about on June 1st 2022, retirement from teaching 21 years at Texas A&M University Corpus Christi and a hospital stay for seven nights. These poems, the emotional and physical fallout of these two events peppered with medicine such as Sertraline that guarantees life but no orgasmic joy, spontaneous and raw whip through the veil as a Jupiterian wind. Scoffing at humanities' follies, while praising the voices of fellow poets, lines here explore the terrain of memory, express the vast presence of travel with an infusion of Greek mythology while exposing the sexualized self and pure failure.

where does love go

Where does love go	1
Song of the Sawdust	2
Hell of a Hand	3
The Great Stew	5
Let me tell you something	9
For the three Student of English met on the Tram in Antalya, Türkiye	11
It takes three to tangle	13
Thank You	14
Negative Capability	16
Palm frond shadows sway	18
South Texas Blues	19
Caught Four Nothings	21
7 23 23 Sunday Fort Defiance State Park	23
when they ask	25
Artemis' Temple	27
Essence	28
Site 13 Revisited	30
Lunch Poem	31
Emmy Pérez in Flight	33
Rotten Floorboards	35
Eclipse Day	37
Drugged Manikin	39
To all the women	40
Where is the Vagabond Poet?	42
Kansas City	44
Dot Vin KYU	46
Numbers and Thumbs	47
I love Michael Rothenberg	49
Monday, over Belgrade	51
Jane, Jeanne and Joan *villanelle*	54
Alan's with me	56
Tantalize	58
Apostrophe Chant	60

Awkward	61
Yes, Barefooted	62
Bro on the Twining	66
desperate	67
Walkin' the fence-line	69
7 8 23 Petaluma	70
Leap Day Poem	72
Troy	74
Krabs	78
Ah, Cosy	81
glade of shadows	83
Dear Daddy Daedalus	85
What Tesla Taught Me	89
Oljato *hibon*	90
This note is my Thank You!	92
"Picked up by a wire"	95
The Ride Home	96
Sonnet V	98
Stressed, Not Stressed, Not	99
In Celebration of International Trans Day	100
Lost it all	101
The Stick	103
Spider Woman Spider-Rock	105
No Exit	106
Vision #23	108
scared	109
Venezia Eve	111
Pilgrimage; B☮	112
York Minister	115
Icarus	116
I started translating Turkish	123
Acknowledgements	**124**

Where does love go

Where does love go when the body dies?
A question I ask as I drive through pitch nights
the turns, curves and semi-trucks do not answer out loud
unless their honks or curses are to lead me to that rest.

If I bounce between here and there sporadically though
thousands of miles apart, what will I find when I
realize that these questions are only stoppers in my mind?
Can I unplug them gently, can I patch up the holes?

Whatever have I done to unfilter the craziness?
That genie bottle nothing compared to Pandora's insides
desperation of hope so muddy ever so slippery
unable to grasp if one even had the hooks to try.

Bolting as thunder claps across the road ahead
and behind, here's another swallow of willful love,
triple the dose. As mobile, as figurative as
the archer's arrow flies to strike me stone dead.

I cannot will not shall not comply with anything but love.

Song of the Sawdust

Listen to the sawdust
Tells trees how to dream:

Sharks may have been here first
But we're swayin' in a breeze.

As long as your roots grow strong
Birds perch & nest on your limbs.

Beetles bite then that old woodpecker
Cleanin' out that chaw'd deadwood;

Housin' life within the dead.
Words that the sawdust sings.

Hell of a Hand

after Woody Guthrie

From the bottom of the deck
The workin' man's gloveless hand was delt.
Stakes too high, skimpy paycheck
Supply chain blowback, lowball cards flipped on the felt.

The boss wrestles me for each and every dollar
Shives my hours and confiscates my tools.
Words of the rich whip up my ire on Parlor
Grinds me into the pavers just to rule.

It's hard to concentrate on my workin' trade
Being told them's our enemies who stole our crumb.
Too much information, and pompous cavalcade
They want us to fight them or become a homeless bum.

Loyalty oaths, nondisclosures signatures only
A rich person would devise.
A *thinking* worker stands apart and lonely
Sifts their words to catch their lies.

Not looking for a handout but seeking relief.
Circus clowns and barkers' pseudo absolution.
The devil by any other clothes exacerbates grief.
Civil insurrection sweetie, "I am your retribution."

Between hammer and anvil lays the worker's card
Business is a Ponzi scheme yoking the worker's neck
Promises of prime cuts are delt as chunks of lard
The worker's worked to death to be discarded dreck.

The Great Stew

I stew, Prue

a great bouillabaisse

medical Iranian saffron infusion

Black Sea cauldron

Bosporus syphon

Scrapping the sweat

    from

        Cami[1]

    chicken blood

        black rock

            walk

            into ink

                that writes

                here

                now

Prue, I stew

    Crimea shoreline

Where are those wheat tankers

    that grew south of Kyiv

        cluster bombs and depleted uranium shells

---

[1] Cami is Turkish for mosque and specifically Suleymaniye Cami

couldn't they be clamming shells, Prue
        off the OBX
               where they grow large?
Or the shells pagan
        of the way
      — on the bridal dress
        baptizing James' arrival
          if you believe
              in
            any of
            that myth

Prue, I stew, Prue,
    proving in the drawer
        rising to the occasion
           laminations obvious
        flaky crust
          above the war
           of the
            Ukrainian
            Holocaust

At the hand of Putin
I stew, Prue,

That teat white hot
  Bosporus choppy
    a bay leaf &
    frankincense
  ground cardamon
     cumin seed
     to pulverize
       a shot of Raki
      Prue please,
         Prue,
      I stew

In rising tides
  In rising temps
    In rising prices
     In rising anger
     In rising expectations
      In rising cremations
      In I, Prue, I stew

My aroma
  Prawns in a boil
    Curry in a bowl

Fresh blood in the streets
        Bodies rotting in the yard

Prue,

    Eat me up

        Before I fester

           Before I mold

              Before my

              Pulchritude

              Becomes putrid,

              I stew, Prue

Into bones and broth

    Savory and hot

    Swallow deep

        Drink to your health

           Prue

        I've stewed and stewed

           Feed you my

              Blood

              Down to

              The marrow

              I stew, Prue

Let me tell you something

Young, I heard love

From the Beatles "Something"

If mint was green and was bright

Shiny layback sleepy time Rambler

At the drive-in with mom

Surprise! I fell asleep

In Sierra twilight, guys having fun

Bare ass sliding on granite

Above Upper Indian Head Falls

Below Howdy's Hole

Our inhibitions

like our youth

    gone

That's the life

One of the best summers

    with my three kids

  Into the land of snow-covered bison

  Chasing moose around the campsite

  Tide pooling the cold Pacific

  Hanging out during the day at home

Always fills me with surprise

  Joy

    That I have

To tell you

Isn't that

Something

For the three Student of English met on the Tram in Antalya, Türkiye

Do the right thang
slang word ending
perfect mantra.

When you helped
other's grow
from the warmth

of your kindness,
"Let me help."
That little bit

of English
heartfelt warmth,
thank you.

Continue your fifty-one
hours of study a week.
To grow—

To help—

You are mighty and kind.

To our new three

friends.

Peace be with you,

Eyvallah.[2]

---

[2]Sufiism slang: I accept your existence

It takes three to tangle

Remember the battle of Anita Hill.

Staring Uncle Thom — ass

and his wife, Long Dong Strap-On.

Senator Chappaquiddick and Queasy Orrin

Mormon left the other four women outside.

Low blow Joe's deal ended Roe vs Wade.

Long Dong left a voice mail:

Apologize! (a supposed olive branch.

Thank You

Sitting on a polished granite slab
at your feet, Muhammad Ali.

A gorgeous yellow and black butterfly
a swallowtail dances about, no bee to be seen

As close as one ever gets to you,
Muhammad, in this life time.

My favorite quote of yours "Looking at life
from a different perspective makes you realize

that it's not the deer that is crossing the road,
rather it's the road that's crossing the forest."

Though I drive those forest crossings in search
of another moment it's hard knowing all

that I've known many cannot. Trying
to keep it real here, Muhammad Ali.

Your wasp arrived landing on the pavers.

Do not tread here if you're not ready to serve.

You're the man. You're the man, Muhammad Ali. Fighting reality. Fighting for justice. Fighting for love and peace.

Thank you, Muhammad Ali

Negative Capability

Tourists' snaps on the Spanish Steps
people watching through the window

from here, at the footboard
of John Keats' deathbed.

Two hundred four years ago
This coming Sunday

Saturday, we touched "This Grave"
of "whose name writ in water."

The crumbling old Roman wall abuts
Caius Cestius' alabaster Pyramid.

Hooded crows cawing to Daisy Miller's ghost
mourning doves murmur odes to the still air.

Will Frances get out of his hospital bed
To bless the Protestant or anyone anymore?

Roam as we may these Polizia streets

automatic lead worms and bores flesh

cars stream outside the living cemetery gates.

Self-indulgent selfie tourist like ourselves

chastised for taking our photo with each of your tombs

a shout out from Keats, Shelley and Corso's graves.

Palm frond shadows sway

Palm frond shadows sway
Typhus in my veins pills to kill
the virus that itches the body all over.

It didn't help when they shaved
my chest, besides ripping the hair
out every time putting on a new

EKG. I get messages: we prayed,
we care, we're wondering if you can
give us your voice, give us your

approval—let people know you are
with us, whether you are or not.
In the shadows of palm fronds dancing;

cannot be captured, cannot be changed
nothing else except dance
until I fall to the ground to die.

South Texas Blues

(five videos while driving)

>While squeezing the zits
>of the soft white underbelly
>of America
>observe
>the racial rashes of untreated
>staph infections of self-loathing
>
>The carrion comet
>beak pluck the putrid festering bodies
>until
>until
>until
>the firebrand liver
>is gone for the night
>grows back
>
>In my mind I staunch the wounds
>by driving these hallow roads
>across America
>reading my poems
>spiriting my words
>greet and meet
>because I'm beat

Beaten down from working
every year since 1977
the year of the punk
and I am just beginning
to be completely free

If I seem lazy
well
I just do the jobs that I want now
that's just the way it is
that's just the way it is
KOOl

Caught Four Nothings

Uncollared wind

Waves up streets

Hills of fire

Magastopo unleased

Corpus palms

    Windblown

        Down Ocean Drive

Cabins of Cape Lookout

    Body surf

    Lookout Bight

Creek flames boil

    Too hot

        Creates meadows

Bumper-sticker-cheddar

        Running red

        Lights-out camps

To say the least

        Pivot and sweep

        A block and a half

        Where dolphins swim

Desktop piles — notebook fresh

Carved back — minimalist stoned

I love swim — that's the wife and I

Her initials and I — sacred word

Planet alignment fifteen days away

Venezia flight weeks after half-mast

Inauguration of the stench cyclone

Back heal up, there's waves to surf

7 23 23 Sunday Fort Defiance State Park

The coming together, confluence
    Of the Ohio & Big Muddy
       Mississippi
Lewis, Clark & William Heat Moon
   Two hundred years
     The rivers
       Upped and moved
          South second street
            —— Cairo
         Training
  Sextant, octant
    Artificial horizon
      First longitude & latitude
    [the breeze chills in the shade
    ramble on, Dude

  Sights and sounds
Steel wheels on rails
Squeaking fierce
Painted rail cars plod along
   Seems steel cannot be

    Remelted and tempered, again

    Metal fatigue suspect

Trucks are everywhere on the interstates

Traffic immense

    Tough roads

        Little Rock to Memphis

        Memphis to Louisville

        Memphis to Asheville

           Orange cones

Humanity's theme song,

      "I love trash"

    Oscar! Oscar!

when they ask

when they ask

you to call them

they and them

it's a no brainer

of course

we love you

follow through

is not so easy

especially in conversation

where the mind accelerates

those old pronouns

blunder into the light

it's not that we

do not respect them

or do not love them

it's remapping the mind

into they and them

whom we love

please have mercy

in this transitional phase

we love them

as they are our own

Artemis' Temple

We traversed trampled dirt among heaped stones
a bush strewn ravine meanders through rough trail

laden landscape that was once Artemis' peripteral temple,
one of the great seven ancient wonders of the world.

All that's left outside Ephesus are scattered blocks and
one lone pillar most likely restacked after the British

pillaged and the locals foraged to make their homes.
There are no guards, no one to pay homage or pray

as one wanders through Diana's verge the Amazonians
first built or the Lydians who quarried Anatolia marble

twenty-eight centuries ago, thereabouts. A micro dose
of ancient occidental history. Antipater of Sidon told

Atatürk, "The Sun never looked on aught so grand."
Where immigrants trod the sand of the great flood.

Essence

Lily, a flower
        rooted in water, Monet
        planted and painted

crush petals release enigmatic aroma
what air of sensation wafts
sweet sniffs of the trail
searching for the source
        led me to you, my darling
            led me to you

one cannot bottle one's essence
for the dealers would be rich of reward
holding you in their hands to deal at will
or give away at a whim without care
how could one's regard be that reckless?

Cannot say, *Tchau*
any more than one can stop glowing

over extended

    encompasses a well

             of essence

those of who have drank

drunk they would fall

but I stagger on

my thirst still wet

Site 13 Revisited

 Tucked between Old Marshall Highway
cataract roars down on the French Broad banks
water flows north across ancient cascades
geese honk intimate call upstream over current
loamy edge water low leaning Canadian Hemlock
                        — overwhelms
tent pitched, fire cracklin' down to coals to cook
away from crowds' eyes, only cardinals and a cony

Helene balled the French Broad into boring new
banks, trunks stuffed cataract roar as speed of light
Old Marshall Highway washed out, train tracks cars
knocked off like Zuma Coffee, as lilacs in bloom
spin in the muddy current with bloating bodies

Lunch Poem

Last sandwich of the loaf
heel and penultimate spread
peanut butter and honey
made yesterday morning

nosh for body surfing beaches
post rain Pensacola's white sand,
Cotton Bayou in Orange Beach, AL.
In Fort Morgan, took the Mobile ferry

to Dauphin Island. Navigate the inlet
of Mobile Bay. West End beach.
Midafternoon waves were too light
for surfing, so floated in the stream.

Now, at the Forester's wheel on Wagner Street,
gorging sandwich, across from Old Bull Lee's place
"The big grab goes on in Washington & Moscow,"[3]
Bill Burroughs' haunt — Algiers Point

In my mind, here with me — PW Covington,
Nathan Brown and Edward Vidaurre.

---
[3] Quote from Jack Kerouac's *On The Road*.

Their overlapping voices cascading
through thick air, as we shamble to the ferry

across the big muddy into the promise of hard
reality, that luscious Quarter of the Crescent City.

Emmy Pérez in Flight

Emmy Pérez writes a poem.
Journal in hand with poem pen

Consults her phone for phrases.
Maybe Emmy Pérez writes notes

on her students' work: suggests
enjambment. Emmy Pérez

steadily arranges words on the page,
journal flat on the tray table

where the flight turbulence
impedes Emmy's graceful pen stroke

air pocket hard smacks
ink askew, Emmy's breath

draws in the N95 black mask
heart leaps as hand scribes

into Houston, "Poets
going down in flames."

Todos mundo caos;
air current quality atmospheric

rivers — winds of Jupiter
pen in hand, one more flight home

en el Valle, Rio Grande.
Emmy Pérez duels through duende.

Rotten Floorboards

Steppin' through rotten floorboards
Breaks the plane painfully.

Lights out Michael Quinn
Em's dad's septic organ shut down.

Don't you catch Covid or Covfefe
Bitch slapped time and time again

Stop in Friday Harbor's The Bean Café
Dance to the metronomic beat

Quiet still moments in an edgy neighborhood.
Kerouac visited Olsen, August 17th 1968.

Killing people to consume chocolate
Eating horseradish pseudo wasabi

Soylent Green next course.
Humanity, I would divorce you

If I could afford each blood payment
A poor wordsmith paid by the cow

Clock's secondhand tick.
Cats' brushings up against 501s.

Lover's head on my rising chest
Gazes' ancient light beams of stars

The illusionist tango of Moon and Sun
As our virus spreads through the Kuiper Belt

Following Hitler's BARK, Bark, bark,   b   arc
Our heart of darkness propelled forever.

Foot sunk through floor — smile and wave, boys
No help on the horizon in our winter's discontent.

Eclipse Day

Twenty minutes before

Sol passes behind moon

Our star Our mistress

Artemis night

for four plus minutes

How far will temperature drop

20-40 percent cloud cover

will we see

with St. Joseph 2017 glasses

The full corona

Extinguished, eight minutes light

Gone in a near blink of Time

and Einstein proved that was reality

on Earth, warping space bodies

until only black holes exist

like the million years it rained

water evaporated from the rock

wept for what was to come

all five existences wipe outs

we surf a limited time in a

liminal place, in Simancas 939

Drugged Manikin

I give you my life

But it's my bag of bones

You want to burn

Feed me clothe me

Shove me through

The charnel house

Propped up now

Drugged manikin

Bleeding puss through pores

How many rounds can

one take with their

flesh shreds flapping

To all the women

To all the women that I have disappointed:
because I wasn't smart enough
sober enough
thick enough
submissive enough
that I couldn't read your coded clues on what
I should be doing precisely at this moment
for you.

To all the women that I've disappointed:
because I wasn't tender enough
rough enough
quiet enough
domestic enough
because I thought more of you than just naked
or eating food and I put these words
onto parchment much to your chagrin.

To all you women, alive or dead, that I've disappointed:
your vivisection of this asunder heart nearly drained
this body of its life blood

but the mind never forgets each

anesthesia free scalpel slice

nerve endings severed or deadened.

To all you women, alive or dead, that I've disappointed:

I still remember you and our times together.

I still love you and I have forgiven you and

myself of these short cummings.

I go in peace, after all

I'm only here a little while.

Where is the Vagabond Poet?

For Nathan Brown

He beams in under the hanging
ten speed

At the table with the classic
green light shade

Notebook laid flat open,
color pens

Strewn about, a black ink pen
in hand

Stroking out a fine poem as the
coffee grows colder, then the switch

A fine laced 100%
agave margarita

And the Vagabond arcs
the current

Into phrases, images and

distinct voices

Going back to redraft the

beginning lines

The hook and then the

final lines

Pop the audience's bubble

With a salud and a deep sip.

Kansas City

Milquetoast America
Decked out in red and gold.
Ribbon hair girls with clear backpacks,
Yoga pants moms with Yeti coffee,
A cold Chiefs Kingdom afternoon.
Super Bowl celebration sans Taylor Swift
DJ shot and kids' blood forever stains fear.

To you American MAGAstopo ingrates
Emigrant's do not jump fences
Swim through roils of barbed wire
To buy guns to kill in mass.
That's the white man's problem
A life of abuse, neglect and lack of love
Become gun toting bullies coveting blood.

In his daily letters, Brady Peterson said,
"Do my poet friends really feel safe at Scissortail?"
Brady, when that lone gunman bursts into Estep,
Bump stock rifle spraying me at the podium
My blood splattering orange and gray paint.

Duck and cover. Remember you fools in paradise,
That there are three exits in this no exit life.

All those young Kansas Swifty girls
Ribbons dangled in the cold breeze of
Small market KC last week, as I watched
Bright innocent eyes come and go pre-
Super Bowl rally with broad smiles across
their faces that excitedly exhale condensation.
Now they bathe in hot sticky copper blood.

Dot
Vin
KYU

weaving　　　round　　　semi-trucks

　　in the bologna belt

　　billboard cleavage

　　draws 'em in

　　North US 49

　　Mississippi

　　Mama Justice

　　Nitro Bomb

Numbers and Thumbs

Stuck

in that paralyzed phase

hours on the john

    playing solitaire

    watching reels

    passing time & gas

Daily Sudoku

numbers and thumbs

mind mindless

    drilling

    deep

goldless settles for quarts

Lapis lazuli

on my hand

in my pocket

a stone in each three rucks

    we prayed

    Euros plunk

    both our hands hold and light

      candle protection

      Hurricane Milton

      to San Antoine

broken only by the shriek of the osprey[4]

      pence paid by the faithful

      Église Saint-Pierre de Montmartre

put the phone down

pick up the pen

glide as if on ice

looking up at Half Dome

---

[4] *The Red and The Black*, Stendhal, p. 457.

I love Michael Rothenberg

I loved Michael Rothenberg's
Usage of Chernyshevsky's
    What is to be done?
    It's Candide for me
    Shut up and work the garden

Tom, Alan said
You're domestic
    Scoop the boxes
    Sweep the floor
    Take out the trash
    Recycling
    Change water
    Feed cats
    Unloaded dishwasher
    Dishes
    Clean and stowed

Susan looks like she's twenty-five
  Rocking my socks
There's a few too many screws loose

I'm not destined for the booby-hatch

The parabola

Through the thatch

    Well-trimmed mons

    Delta of Venus

    Fixated

    Shaking now

    With cold

Walking

    Writing

        I stand

Monday, over Belgrade

Mevlâna Karenina[5]
whirling in the sun
are you grounded?
Centered, counter clockwise
right hand skyward
left hand earth bound
"He glanced at the sky [...] I love her."

Whirl on Mashkin Hill. "Sun [...]
sinks beyond" the woods. Scythe
in hand, Mevlâna Matt Sedillo
Mowing Leaves of Grass.[6] Whirling
swaths of Colonia grass in awe.
We watch the Alighieri laurels twirl,
whirl, mowing Colonia grass.

As if Levin — "Sharp scythe [...]
whizz through juicy grass." Mevlâna
Pearl. Mevlâna Girl. Mevlâna world.

---

[5]Mevlâna is known in America as the poet Rumi; Karenina comes from Leo Tolstoy's novel *Anna Karenina* as well as all quotes unless otherwise indicated.

[6]Book of poems by Matt Sedillo.

"Can't we all just get along?"[7]
Two things, my friend. First, respect
your wife. your daughters, your fellow females
no more cover ups: metal band Bahrain burkas

hajibs, bikinis, except for sickness.
Second, my friend, go ahead, sip your tea
I brewed it just for you! Yes, yes, second.
Self-control. What?! Yes, self-control
of yourself. Keep your hand out of other's
cookie jars. Smile, nod, keep those lascivious
thoughts to self or pen and paper or if you can

render them as art. Now whirl
counter clockwise my friends
whirl as we always spin our vortex
spiraling through galactic dark matter brine.
Into the transferential trance, transcendental
higher plane. Tap like a beet root, like a maple
tree, like a palm wine. Use your mental spile.

Transfiguration, bridge the gap

---

[7]Rodney King.

as Mevlâna Karenina bridges time.

Shams[8] spoke, "Give me *bi mola*.[9]
Transformative: *Eyvallah*[10]
touch right hand to heart.
Eyvallah. Ahoalton.[11]
Eyvallah Ahoalton.

---

[8]Shams was Rumi's mentor
[9]Turkish: a break
[10]Sufiism slang: I accept your existence
[11]Lenape word: To love one another

Jane, Jeanne and Joan *villanelle*

Martin Luther, war protests—the news drones
Three kids saddled housewives, their husbands pricks
Jane and Jeanne drink afternoon wine with Joan

Husbands drink all night in the titty zone
Copenhagen Theater all nude chicks
Moon shot, Mi Lai Massacre—the news drones

Military service plane crash alone
Weapons full duffle bag, Dumbarton fix
Jeanne in black cloth mourns, Jane drinks wine with Joan

New Zealand bound husbands with Jane and Joan
Colonel said, "I would shut her damn mouth quick."
Ayatollah Hostages—the news drones

Sculpture wood carver never makes it home
Shacked up with young broad who favors lipstick
Jane and Jeanne drink vodka tonics with Joan

Husband looks at fat wife and calls her crone

Man beckons young admin, takes her hand, licks

AIDs, the Berlin Wall falls—hear the news drone

Heavy smoker, drinker, abuser prone

Lymphatic cancer eighteen months indicts

Jane weeps for freedom, Jeanne drinks wine with Joan

"Bathhouse fisting," conservative Jeanne moans

Smash car Joan, almost dead drunk bailiwick

Nine Eleven, Wall Street crash—the news drones

Dead Jane and dead Joan, Jeanne finds own tombstone

Alan's with me

Alan's been a pillar in my life
even before I knew him, I knew him.

Protesting woman yelled,
"Check their IDs,"
as we bought tickets for Caligula.
Seventeen with fake temporary license.
I shook in fear but
Alan Berecka was there with me.

Lights off, Alan laughed
as the Ford LTD spun doughnuts
on the Terman Junior High
lawn and splashing through giant
mudpuddles. Alan's giggle slides out
like one of his jokes or repartees.

I slipped on water and landed flat
on my back. Alan pulled me up
by my jockstrap and shook
off the dust and slapped my ass

with a new poem that hit the marrow

as a sucker punch to a bloated gut

Alan has always been with me.

Even before emailing and calling

for poetry events he organized.

It took a few years for me to attend

that butterfly effect that went,

"Hey Tommy, did you hear the one about…"

Alan Berecka will always be with me.

Tantalize

Sunburn forehead gotten
waiting in a freezing lake
for you to join in the cold

waiting to see your nipples
harden through the padding
of your bikini top. Too thick

for my taste. An' that full ass
sexy as fuck. Man, could sink
teeth in. Almost completely

lost it — your high crotch
mons for my eyes. You said,
I'm a sharp observer. I note

it all. The skirts & dresses.
An' so scared to be burned
Again, but my attention excites

you, play safely. Control, cautious,
curious, yearn for touch, knowing safety first.
What would I do? Oh, dream it darling

dream the ocean's wide, dream waves
oscillations, undulations. Dream the smile
that will take you through dawn to twilight.

Your name on my tongue tip slides
around until you quake and cum.

Apostrophe Chant

apostrophe chant
      Bring back Pico[12]

  we're dying for a look
      at his liver

---

[12] Pico della Mirandola (1463-1494)

Awkward

Tongue cut off
grew again
speaking
off the cuff

Honky discourse
all I've unknown
conduct myself
as other

other than my sex
other than my skin
other reclaimed

Kids laugh at what is awkward
not knowing or understanding
laugh out their
lack of knowledge

curiosity helps free you
from xenophobia
laugh and learn, child
learn and love

Yes, Barefooted

Barefooted, yes
like Hilary & Ronald

Tolkien in Sarehole
Running paths from the mill

To River Cole and Mosely Bog
Like myself in Matadero Creek

Edging the donkey pasture
Along the old railroad line

Bonemeal Sarehole Mill
Matadero slaughterhouse

Cool clear water trickle
Down towards Driftwood

Market. Being chased off
Out of someone's backyard

Rattling fence staves
Like Hilary & Ronald by

The Miller's son they called
The 'White Ogre.' There was an

Ogre riding unicycles and swinging
Through trees to fort platforms

Ropes high in ancient creek side oaks,
Running on fence tops playing off

The ground tag and later, smoking
Pot on a waterbed in blacklight

Homemade backyard fort. Being
groomed for a camping rape.

Ronald and Hilary's White Ogre only
Wanted to beat, not beat their meat.

And like the Tolkien boys lost adventures
Sarehole the Shire or Hobbiton

Mosely Bog's stinky wet trail
Near captures, by the Old Forrest

By the evil outsider Nazgul
The inner ogres and the evil war

Lurked and line every open field or lot
Picking off individuals, seducing others

For the cause of progress, a good
Life in silicone, tobacco and heady

Drink to wallow away and rejoice
In the good moment away from

The advertisements, glorifications and
The Vietnam body-bag count or the

Invasion of the Beatles when
They played their last stadium

And bedded down at Cabaña House
Just a wee babe[13] barefooted

On long grass across the street
Worrying of the bees' death

---

[13] Babe pronounced as bab

Sting as they came to clover
Flowers in the evening gambol

Like you, Hilary and Ronald Tolkien
In respective Shires of our minds.

Yes, barefooted.

Bro on the Twining

Hey bro, on the Twining Tree Farm
How does your sweet bonnie lass bake go?
Me self, better than turf peat smoked dry
I almost sang the Sky Boat song
turnkey sawbones patched me 'just' enough
out the gate soon, down along the water banks
till home rest and rest, the rest is up to me,
my bro on the Twining Tree Farm.

desperate

desperate
the party in two days
I cannot come
  Susan
tight blue skirt
   black tights
    Jesus
long ways on the arms
   comes to mind
razorblades
   that's the quickest

so, I get stoned
writing poetry, again
   Jesus
the thoughts in my head

I even thought about Grindr
   for a blowjob
   and the heart?
I could be AFib now

no difference
    need another
    one twenty-five
joules   Jesus

still falling
    off the KS
dumpster
rock bottom
    coming
        down / up

Walkin' the fence-line

post to post
security uniform pocket
hand researching
pocket payoff

[other side of cyclone]
SWAT rifle through brush
helicopter overhead
'84 Olympics

opening night
unfolding
Stanford campus
grabber grabs

soft stone pipe
bowl packed
mid walk pause
flick my Bic

flight
cross check
fly

7 8 23 Petaluma

Spider threads

Complex simple

Woven in the dark

Glisten in the light

Tethered to wind

Snares to feed

How all is woven

Threads, cells, elements

Chemicals to sense

Japanese maple boughs sway

Reaching for sunlight

In the easterly cold dawn

Sharks older than first trees

Above the shoreline

Younger growth

In idle time thought

Curiosity, inlaid on

An invisible web

All the trees now cabinets

Armoires, chairs

Banister on wooden

Deck where spiders spin

On my thoughts

Collecting feeding

Leap Day Poem

Leap over the oncology form

Disclose information to other

Living wills, DNR type attorney

Leap over Steph's inflamed kidneys

One three times normal size and

Shutting down her appetite

Leap over the Texas size wildfire

No one raked the panhandle awaiting

The ten-foot snowfall in the Sierras

Leap over two presidents on the border

One in power but powerless the

Other a douche bag in a racist park

Leap over back pain subluxation

Ice and heat, ice calving lava flows

Atlas guilt instead of punting

Leap over the brazen lies, the

scam artists using USPS and the

Border Patrol claiming strange activity

Leap over Bob Kaufman, Richard

Brautigan, Hunter S. Thompson

Into the lonely heartbroken souls

Leap over Grasmere Lake District

Leap over string vibration dimensions

Leap over my open waiting grave

Leap with arms wide open

Leap with heart beating fast

Leap with dark sky eyes feasting

Troy

    Seeing sheep in sleep
        — their sad-grey
            worth.
    If one was plucked
    from Paris' flock
    Helen
    would launch
    infinite ships.
    Beggars on the shore
    demand Cassandra
    ruffle sails —
    conjure a storm.
    A wooden horse.
    A Senate impeachment.

    Bring out the
        witness.
    Bolton so bright
    mustache monogram.
A Bush babbling idiot —
        douche bag deluxe.

    Shockingly, might not be a
        liar
   only a cyclopean
      fool.

Oh Penelope,
        weave me
   a shroud
   warp and woof
   me into
the Ferryman's boat.

Oh Poseidon,
     what did you do
     with Hart Crane's
     cock?

Gave it to Narcissus.
    Marry it to Atlas.
    Hand it to Prometheus,
    to wander down the
        mountain
    to light a woman's
        fire.

Oh Negritude,
> give me Zora's mouth
>
> Kobe's heart and
>
> Henry Ozawa Tanner's
>> brush stroke.

Oh Sitting Bull,
> give me Black Elk's voice
>
> Geronimo's reins
>
> and Spider Rock's
>> spiritual
>>> vortex.

Oh parents,
> give me your survival
>> skills
>
> your shotgun weddings
>
> your alabaster
>> nothingness.

And you,
> Dorothy and Devey.

And you,
> Alice and Alan.

And you,

      Larry and Lisa.

And you,

      Alan and Annie.

Give me strength.

Give me strength

      to wake

      once more

      in the

      morn

      to staunch

      these wounds

      before helping to

      shove

      that wooden horse

      inside the gates.

Krabs

Twenty fourth anniversary of Ma's passing
After 3.17 miles on the elliptical

I think of Krabs
Him & David Losé
On bikes
Baring down on me
Infront of the music room
At Terman Junior High
David, nun chucks in waistband
yelling, Murphy

David dead by end of term
[That's another Story
Krabs honored with
The first David K. Losé
Award for athleticism
Jack Kerr the second
Before Jerry Garcia asked
"Long distance runner,
    what you holdin' out for?"

Krabs and I continued to wrestle
He caught me observing him

Picking his teeth
He said,
Pussy hairs.
I laughed like ink & dink
Around the Gunn campus
Krabs would see me and pick his teeth
I always laughed

By the gym side
Of the parking lot
Where Dewark's battery
Exploded
Krabs talked with a cutie
Through her car window
Bummed a smoke
Just after wrestling practice
I was too athletically
Religious
Saw it as a sacrilege
Little did I know
This morning

I did the same
At the Casa del Palmas
Hotel in McAllen, Texas
On the third floor balcony

Touching a leaf of the banyan tree

In the patio

Having an American Spirit

@ six thirty am

And when Krab's girl Becky

Took a shower as he waited in her home

With her friend Anne who

Got down on her knees

Blew him

Thank you very much

Krabs

For the fantasy

That has played on

From the player himself

A kind man

That I only knew

From the past

Hurling through space

Spiraling

Around the sun

For the sixty second time

Ah, Cosy

Ah, Cosy,
    The stones we touched.
I imagine you now leaner, tramping
best maps take you into war zones
hefting an RPG through building rubble
fighting for water and warmth in Ukraine.

Remember rolling smokes on the outside table
of the Red Lion's beer garden in the middle
of the North Henge, the Sun Henge of Avebury?
Wadsworth 6X our mutual pints as we were wiled
in simpler times. Though you roll with gritty fingers
in the dark since Putin's strafing has snuffed out

light. Ah, Cosy, I'm afraid
to email you again, afraid to receive
your silent death in response. I'm afraid
our assent on Silbury, our walk through
the mound and around the Sarsens, mere pipe
dream before constant bombardment explodes.

Ah, Cosy, the world is full of hate
while others get rich and drink
their profits with babes' blood.
Things fall apart, but to expect
a deus ex machina; ludicrous.
That ungodly light blinds.

glade of shadows

Plato faux dances
the Socratic hemlock
on the edge of Windmill Hill
stage dives into the pits

where wench pulls and pushes you
towards the flames
in front of the plinth obelisk

      "Keep me warm   burn my hands"

Abbot Ale brewed last Sunday
Monday felt like Pleiades scourge
Tuesday, was there ever a Mars day worse
Wednesday, such an imp, call her *duende*
Thursday thunderstorm — drench my mutated
      mouth with axe cuts and dank slate
Freitag's snail dance howl — slow
      conjure, weaving a yarn-poem
      below the metal weft of Ruth Asawa
Saturn's Day, moody waters break against stone

Sun day, Domingo Live, creeps into ancient shade
        your meander yanks me
              under
shake bones   rattle snake
writhe a path

shake sway   rattle
       bones
like the steppin' round
       acid drip eyes

rattle bones   shake moan
       gnawing bowels

            jump   bones
rattle shake

       pierce your nook
  writhe groan   raw

Dear Daddy Daedalus

Thirty-one years ago, to the day
You died
Heartbroken
    But expected
        The yoke
            Lifted

Five days earlier
    The last time
        I wished you Happy Birthday
            USMC

Daddy: Mr. Vice
Mot: Long live the United State and success to the Marines
All: The Corp
Daddy: Mr. Vice
Mot: The President of the United States of America
All: The President
Daddy: Mr. Vice
Mot: The House
All: The House

    And I wished you Happy Birthday
        You looked confused

As you lay dying
In front of me

The 1970 photo
    Of you and ma
    You nearly forty-one
    Ma at thirty-three
    Christmas time
    Down at eight
    I knew already
    Your brute force
    And sexualized mind
        Conjuring me
        To tell tales
    Your gratification
    Wasn't apparent
    Learning about hard and soft
        With a slap
        Backhanded

My first tales
Sexual in nature

Thirty-one years
Over half my life
You've been dead
I scattered you and Ma
Stoneman's Meadow

I've tried to let go
      But it's difficult
      In the labyrinth
      You made
      That I tread
      Your mug in 70
      That grin
      Crewcut pate
      After a cocktail
      Look even happy
      A distinctive face
      Kind of like
           My own
 Blue eyes
Nobody else in our family had

The Iceman's Child
And Alice
Those were names
You called me

I can still hear you
      Calling my name
      Running to you
      For a beating

I've never hit

        Susan

        Rowan

        Anna

        Ellie

One thing

    I can smile

        About

Peace and love, Dad

PS Don't forget

    You're the first

    To associate myself

    With sin and vice

    And made me pay

    For screwing up

    Your life

Peace and love, Dad

What Tesla Taught Me

buy cheap sell high
automated transportation
trans intelligence mixing
Sapiens and machines
where the latter refuses assimilation

AI becoming the lead pipes in Rome
We have our Nero fiddling the Tariff fling
Waiting to ink a golf course in Gaza
Along with casino and the ultimate Americanism
Strip malls with Shekel Stores

Oljato *hibon*

Hot fire from US 168 down
into the meadow forest
burned trees, cones and seeds

Only on the perimeter of
green and brown do new
pines and firs regenerate

Sierra Lupin field of purple
lanyards abundant life,
Pileated woodpecker pair flit

About down logs for bark
beetles, fly catchers, wood-
peewee and the evening call

Of the Osprey at lake's edge
then dive into the cove in
search of a meal. Scouts

Everywhere, making their way
to and from adventures. Vanilla
smell Jeffery Pine — Oljato Pine.

Oljato thrives, teaming ants,
teaming Scouts. I left my youth
here, forged, tempered, barely

enough to get through the years
but enough to realize that here,
under the largest tree in camp,

the fortune of life
grows and diminishes
moment to moment.

    change is inevitable
    embrace and enjoy
    slow to winter

This note is my Thank You!

Thank you for your kindness
    to let me into
    your lives
    besides
        the cat yowls
    wanting freedom
        from the bedroom —
    ornery thing

stacked tabbies
    carpet platforms
        switch aroo
stocks
    tail High
They're more interesting
    Than
    Stop the wars
    Stop climate change
    Stop Trump
Pirate radio
    Broadcasting
    Channel Z
    I'm alone
/
Not alone lone
    here with the collective
    skimming grounds
        far and wide
    Why — Thank You!
        On your farms
        Lake house   cats
            Casita International District hum
        Green chilis over tatter tots
        TATANKA Buffalo

                      and
                      for a loner – Mik
                                  you sure can
                          Talk
Write it at night
          Thank You!

Dear Covid Friends
Golden cottonwoods
          Aspen
          Rabbit bush
Across the SJV
Thank You!

Enid in the Biv
      Hunky Jesus
      left hand
      holds
      stars
      Tungels
        Stellar
            Estrella
/

Rosemary Pleiades
      Broadcasting Lon Simmons
          with the count
 pass through kitchen
      fuselage garage
      yellow wings
      strapped
      under patio roof
      galvanize
        echo
      rain pouring
           pavers seeping
Thank You!

I saw some gorgeous
                Land
    Colors changes
    Sumac
    Aspen
    Cotton wood
    Rabbit brush
    Heart still beating
    At 10,000 feet
        Okay 8,500
    Thank You!

Woman
That I love
    So much
Thank You!

"Picked up by a wire"
            Hunter S. Thompson *Hells Angels* (p. 72)

Wire fiber optic endless wireless
A world woven warped and woofed
As glistening spider strands billowing
In the morning light reflected off segments
Luminous flashes naturally under wispy clouds
And yet AI now will tap those wireless lanes of data
And control, our coming and goings—they couldn't do
    Any worse than us

The Ride Home
For Carol Coffee Reposa

Exiting Bill S. Cole UC with a box of unsold books
in hand, I glance about the friends I'm leaving here

in Ada, Oklahoma, at East Central U, though Carol
isn't among those chatting, doddering in the afterglow

of another perfect Scissortail Creative Writing Festival.
As I walk out into the fresh air and take my books to the car

Carol isn't around, smoking one of her Doral Lights 100s
from the gold box, slipping me a cig with her impish grin

as if our secret shared was light and giddy as helium inhaled.
The red bud not as brilliant as last year's bloom — difference

of days of winter to spring — alone I pack up the Forester
get my bearings: top off gas, set GPS map up on the phone

turn up Heroin by Lana Del Rey for the ride home. Last year,
Carol disagreed how to leave Ada. I bypassed the Chickasaw

Turnpike, turned around, then we had our only argument.
My dear Carol was a luddite. That's about as nicely put

as I can muster. I cannot count the troubles with her email,
she didn't use her cell phone, couldn't collate her manuscript

computer files — I Did what I could and sent off *Sailing West*
to Katie Hoerth at Lamar University Literary Press. I owed
    Carol.

When she took Susan, Elanor, our five cats and I in, fleeing
Hurricane Harvey. Her kindness overwhelming, though
 quietly

Ellie complained about no Wi-Fi — Carol was hardwired.
Carol dedicated *Sailing West* to her students and me,

her "special friend and Guru." In private, she called me,
"My prince." Her straight black hair, her overweight build,

Carol reminded me of my mom. I not only drove Carol to
Scissortail, but to Granbury for the Langdon Review

Weekend, dropping Carol off at Charles and Dominique Inge's
Brazos House as Texas Poet Laureate, where her hosts
 toasted with Prosecco.

The ride home, Carol, isn't always pretty or tidy as driving
for hours to our resting places. The ride home, Carol, is full

of anger, loneliness and regret. I shall never reveal your
 secrets
or your state of being this past year — Carol, you were under

siege until the end. I last saw you five days before passing,
kissed your forehead, as Thelma witnessed, after I read you

your poem, "Signing the Will." Good night, sweet Carol,
as our paths diverge, we must travel alone on the ride home.

Good night, Carol. May your journey in the sky boat radiate
your light. So, in time, I may follow your vast illuminations.

Sonnet V

Accomplishment today, asked by anyone who cares
Yes, you've retired, how do you spend the sunlit hours

Moon and stars, flicker as space debris crashes atmosphere
Burn to cinder while sitting here at my desk of splotched ink

Smile to view relics of past life lived — living
Proof motor skills continue to arc and scratch thatch through

Isolated from living rough, stealing meals, cult of the cross
Nugs and kisses for all willing to taste sap from a bristlecone

Inside Bachelard's clam shell, driftwood, quartz, seed pod and
    chert
To wood & to stone, older than I knew, younger than zinnias

Basking love, questions beg emptiness dissipate or vaporize
Movement continuously, until pinned down as a beetle
    sideshow freak

'Fire before water' written in charcoal across forests
As plastic cancer attacks earth and sears aching eyes

Stressed, Not Stressed, Not

The potter, the publicist, the porter, the placebo,
I have none of these. If I am not stressed

am I dead? Early morning heat and humidity
hits your chest like a paver thrown by Mad Bum.[1]

You want to leave but will only wander.
The dove coos' line the broken air

into parts per million that's unbreathable.
Tests come back negative QR code.

Words of my childhood have become
Corporations, amazon, yahoo and google.

If you learn the grid does your algorithm
change? Disappear? When you visit Greenville,

Tulsa, will you smell blood? Hear echoes of screams?
Neither were present at Wounded Knee or Guernica

or Teotihuacán. Why do I want to visit Sand Creek?
To learn from history so it doesn't happen again?

Stress has gotten you nowhere.
Thank goodness I am woke.

---

[14] Fan nickname of Madison Bumgarner who won the 2014 World Series MVP for the San Francisco Giants

In Celebration of International Trans Day
(for Rowan)

Once you realize who you are
Changing your pronouns led to a new name
Hormones with Walgreens' blowback, still they persist
To move into your body that matches your mind
Your heart, your soul, and whole being
Readying for top surgery and fancying a beard
Becoming unfettered and at peace
The community embraces you all LGBTQI2S+
Love is Love and life is yours to live
Designated March 31st nonetheless every day
Celebration of the person you've become
Grow into these legs, trunk, arms and head
Lock arms in arms and march your pride

Lost it all
after Allen Ginsburg

Goodbye breath
    Goodbye light
        Wave and particle

Goodbye thundering
    Spring Break
        Yosemite Falls

Goodbye kissing my love
    Goodbye hugging offspring
        Grow and prosper my young ones

Goodbye tweeting cardinals
    Flash your redness
        Through my lost vision

Goodbye geese honking flights
    Glide overhead as I
        Once stood and watched

Goodbye gas pedal that I punch
    Across states
        Across time

Goodbye body that prefers
    Connecting senses
        On the timeline of life

Goodbye thumbs that hold so much
    Opening, putting clothes on
        Snapping off stovetop light

Goodbye youth,
    Goodbye middle age
        Goodbye dotard man.

Hello flames
    Hello salt water
        Hello quantum realm

The Stick

May '71 invited for Rusty Berthume's ninth birthday party
Giants vs the Dirty Dodgers at Candlestick Park—The Stick
Having heard it was in the ghetto, cold as hell
At night when the fog rolled in ready to freeze
We went. Steve Stone pitched, Willy Mays
And Chris Spire hit home runs and the Giants won
Eight to six through a mellow evening in my
White t-shirt and no jacket — what a blast!

October '81 I paid fifty dollars to Rich Berry
For a ticket to see those decrepit thirty-nine-year-olds
The Rolling Stones at the Stick. Sunday ticket, we
Encamped in the parking lot where the party went
All night long with Harry & Erik's coke supply
Where I razor bladed The Who emblem before they
Took it all away. George Thorogood opened then the
J. Geils Band before the Stones rocked out bare tits.

January '90 buying a pack of smokes near Union Square
Sign says, $100 for a 49er's championship game ticket,
I paid it on the spot. The night before, TB and I got
Together with paints and loose canvas and cocaine
What we painted cannot be remembered and too
Wet to travel on the SamTrans bus to the Stick.
Arrived exhausted, lack of sleep, crabby at first, but a
Quick nap before Ronnie Lott knocked the ball
From Flipper Anderson to set the tone for the win.

June '94 as we, Susan, Merritt, Kim and Kay
Crested the second deck to see the Giants take on the
Atlanta Braves when the announcer said, "The inaugural

Poetry in the Park is pleased to introduce our first poet Allen Ginsberg on the pitcher's mound." The jumbotron Sparkled with Ginsberg in his traditional black suit with Vest, white shirt & long black tie launching into "Hum Bom" Who we gonna bomb? where you gonna bomb? The booing, Allen's jumbotron image snapped off, I on the second deck like Dale Arden's Flash Gordon arm motions, yelling "Go, Allen, Go!" The four eyed sissy threw the ball down the pipe.

Spider Woman Spider-Rock
Na'ashjé'íí Asdzáá Tse na'ashje'ii

Escorted only with respect
Diné Canyon de Chelly back bench
en plein air, cast off army truck
through thick sand rivulets into valley
sandstone towering walls sacred space
an invader seeking an unfolding there she was
taller than any obelisk that natural pronged pinnacle
Spider Woman Spider-Rock   weaves
across the valley into sky   weaves
time life and death met out thread
into complex cosmos touches each finger
web shot like Spider-Man Rocked by the Shocker
after desert hail storm machete watermelon
below your base presence. Nourished cool
sweet red crunchy fruit and shy to gaze upon
the goddess that weaves all together
with reverence, my thoughts place me
at your stone skirt   stargazing
To look up and gaze Spider Woman Diné
Guide my eyes, guide my feet, guide us all

No Exit

On my way to Via da Borgo
a courtier of the papal court
wafts Cupid Cologne
phlegmy eyed high
in his footsteps to
courtesan Imperia

Raphael's Galatea upper right stare
robed red crimson over left shoulder
right arm twisting across the bod
bare forehead to hip pulling dolphins
bearing arms triple cupids aim to shoot in love
heart yearns anticipating Galatea's Imperia moan

I always thought myself smart
now I doubt that was ever true
constant yank of impending doom
no parlay cartoon docs
less matrix than chains
of our own making

Silos' philosopher king refusal to clean
in that lawlessness first week of Dis
face shot head down in the gutter
my microns will dis-matriculate
feed a host of maggots
thinking, didn't I see you

at the burning of Savonarola
a howling bonfire of the vanities
Rosalynn's facial expression

turning to unfresh me
like a hot knife to her side
seven days on the road
in the skirts of Hurricane Hugo
at Maranatha Baptist Church
in Plains, Georgia with
Jimmy, Rosalynn and me
having left Imperia in NYC
all I got was an 8x10 3D photo

O Rafael, how can one ride the dolphin
Jeff Koons answered—be the dolphin

Vision #23

When the machines

 whup the Wookiees,
our bones
will have been grounded to dust
for billions of years.

As our star supernovas

in some garden party
across the universe
one will point
to our exploding gasses

to say, "Oh baby, let's shag."

scared

This summer
Mammoth Pools on Big Creek
above Huntington Lake
rocking back and forth
like a 1st year scout
back in '73
Finally letting go
leaping off
      kickoff rock

Rocks look too close
fridged water
mathematics of jump
would momentum be enough
invasion
fish world
cool water swallows
      submersion

Relief
breast stroke to waterfall
cascade always different pattern
climb onto the rocks
clinging tight
      up to a towel

When did I become scared
after the hospital
after leaving Michael Rothenberg
to drive down backroads
Tallahassee to Pensacola
a pass nearly not made
cutting off the truck

oncoming car driving road edge
      waiting for impact

When did I learn to distrust my body
to make it to the can
pissing self
playing kick the can
on La Calle
on Paul Avenue
after hours of driving
pissing in a bottle
      not stopping each hour
Wisdom not real
learned behavior
touch the black conical coil
burns the flesh
will that stench cloud
broil out of stacks
in South Texas
some say the threat not real
others found ways north and south
      pondering here in Corpus

Magastopo proud boys
march in black and gold
in the name of purity and Christ
want to round up my son
      I know why I'm scared.

I have always been scared
Though at times I leap than look

Venezia Eve

to rake to sweep
perfect stance and motion
transfer dowel to synchronize muscle movement
brain pan cookin'

Rose-Ringed Parakeets' crying flights
A green named for their long tails splayed
between internal antiquity wall pock marks
Terme di Caracalla e il Coloseo

Just gotten home
Raking twigs and leaves
What do you do for love
Besides crack Robert Creeley's text

Scout labyrinthine stone lanes bridging canals
Chill Venezia Eve in sea green parka
knit blue Scottish scarf wraps nuzzle neck
vanilla white ski cap's black gondolier stripes

after langostino pesto risotto and single glasses of chianti
Oh, the wine, the wine we tasted and drank
Earthy legs running down Murano glass
Thoughts of the Galleria Borghese mythological tit show
Her smile though footsore and cranky man needs a bier
Selfie gorgeous saying, "I love that you like to travel"

Sweep of her blue eyes
Mine rakes her naked form
Pivot and switch for love
Sweep and rake transfer the dowel

Pilgrimage; B☮

Beat Hang Bolinas
    B☮

nasturtium orange flower vines under
eucalyptus stand canopy
ivy long up trunks
        dharma bum
                Tom
                I met
                with Mary

6 Terrace
        Richard Brautigan lived
                shot his brains out
            12 gauge
        "Messy, isn't it."
        Supposedly wrote
        Ianthe said
            No.

Whalen, Philip baby
                      Zen
Ferlinghetti on the mesa
        Where he wrote
Francis & Joel
        out for a stroll
        overlook B☮

    like
underwear dad
            shirtless
  on front porch
      squatting down
        helping

                his
                        naked
                                    child
        ride
        kiddo bike

speckled fawn & two does
mesa non outlet
        B☮ Gomorrah
        SF Sodom
                surf
                        fog
                                    cypress
        because
                she
                        loved
                                me
                                high

B☮
        drive against the one way
        for parking spot
        barbed wire
        no line horizon

        Beat Hang B☮
        gothic anarchy
                old Chinese woman
                        ghost
                    Richard
        went out
                like Papa
                        PopGun
                                Hemingway

        Pelicans glide
                rows of waves

      surf roar
         kayak paddle

Yak board
there's always
    an undertow
    who or what
      to trust

    better back up
      out of B☮
    too old too young
      Paradiso
        speed hump
        oars out of lock
        w/ **Beat Hang B☮**

    Bolinas Community
            Center
B☮ CO CE

    Food bank Thursday
    Banco de alimentos jueves
      11:00 am
    Elders and disabled
    Ancianos y diseapalitdeos
      11:00 am
      Everyone
      Todas
      SF Marin
      Food Bank

    old hippies gathering
    for their weekly allotment
      thank you
      B☮

York Minister

Fine crenulations flying buttresses gothic orations
Paypal prayers payout for Elon Musk's pocket change
Thirteenth century organ player's name tops the organist
    plaque

Enough Jesus freaking stain glass to satisfy even Jack
    Kerouac
The tourist come and go humming the baselines from Figaro
From the depths of Shaman Siobhan's corner turned horned
    staff

To the point this poem has no center to reference anymore
A man's ringtone Zeppelin's Communication Breakdown
Pub bingo drinking Timothy Taylor's Landlord, lordy how

We all come into this Petri dish a mess dubbed Earth
River Ouse overflows her banks with muddy waters
Onward to Oxford where orcs cut down Tolkien's tree

Behavior nearly ubiquitous point in case laughing dog
    Thrump
John Taylor football player, John Taylor world traveler
Egyptologist teacher and river guide heads to Uzbekistan

Fine handwriting for poems and doctor's letters for treatment
Doctor, give us one more velvet hour[2] — please
Let them forget the hammers of the Yorkshire Ripper

---

[15]Morrison, James Douglas. "An American Prayer"

Icarus

I

I have soared
long before the hijacking
when my body revolt broke through
the brainpan's cockpit door.

Full throated tabid blare
"Something is really wrong with me.
I can hardly stand. My urine's
apple juice infused with rust."

Smart Susan valet the car at the ER
I didn't speak. Susan was my mouthpiece.
My wobbles gained me two attendants who
immediately ushered me into a room and onto a bed.

Told then what I could: ten-day fever,
the day chills, the night sweats.
"There's a mark on my foot
with little red dots around it."

"That could be Typhus or nothing."
Inner elbow needle vein IVs,
couldn't drink enough water,
astronomically parched.

Promethean spark:
"BP's 180 over 140 —
heartbeat's erratic."
At least they didn't cut my clothes off.

Over the seven days in Telemetry
Susan spent every night;
I love her for that.
The trifecta synergy:

Typhus, Pneumonia, A-Fib.

Esophageal Electrical Cardioversion
one hundred twenty-five joules.
"Clear!" restart the heart.

II

"Did I tell you they shaved my chest?"

III

These wings are singed, crispy

orange dots
glide on air currents
around the ceiling light
again & again.
Best hallucination ever.

Janus, el doctor del corazón
uno cara habla, "You can do anything."
La otra cara ofrece, "I wouldn't drink Tito's and Red Bull."

At times, thoughts end up jumbled
or crassly rock-bottom Maslow.
"Did I crap today?" After lunch, time to nap? Write?"

"How'd I almost died? Does it matter, really?"

Gassed, takeoff:

soaring—again
system—indicators
warnings—keep sounding
unable—reach orgasm
constant—diarrhea
unable—to write

and the inconsistent images
flashing in the mind.

First, late November,
breaking down boxes with a box cutter knife.
Go longways on the arms
to insure.

Second,
Miami January
reading *Lady Chatterley's Lover*
on the 19th floor bedroom balcony.
Just hop the rail.
I ran back inside
Locked the glass door
and left the room.

IV

Grateful Dead and Lana Del Rey
playlist downloaded.
I'm falling apart,

taken off,
hijacked,
communications off
flying low over ocean
earth area:
no satellite coverage
    no radar
    no shipping lanes
    no drones fly by
    nobody knows.

Wings melting, asymptotic glide.
Sun rays' glisten on the waves,

knowing the end near,
soar to glide; another splash.

My broken candelabra limbs,
flame quenched salted wounds.

"Oh Poseidon, let great white shark,
Kaaipai, feed upon my flesh. Take my

black box into their gullet and
devour me whole."

So, I may drift, flutter, rotate and descend
down to assimilate with the seabed floor.

To fulfill the prophecy of Daedalus,
my father — 'You little shit.'

"I started translating Turkish"

I started translating Turkish
Işçi Sözü
Workers' Promise newspaper

The best line by N. Cemal
Bariş cezalandirilamaz
There's no punishment for peace

Acknowledgements

Ah, Cosy; Palm Fronds Sway; and **Awkward** in *Corpus Christi Writers 2023*. Corpus Christi, TX. September 2023.

Edward Chillida's "Elogio del Horizonte" en Gijón, España in *3Elements Review*, Issue No. 15, Online. Summer 2017. (cover photograph)

Emmy Pérez in Flight in *Boundless Anthology*. McAllen, TX. April 2025.

The Great Stew in *The Windward Review: Revolution*. Vol. 22. Corpus Christi, TX. October 2024.

Hell of a Hand in *The Working Man's Hand: Celebrating Woody Guthrie-Poems of Protest and Resistance-2023*. Fine Dog Press, July 2023.

It takes three to tangle in *Switchgrass Review*. Corpus Christi, TX. June 2023.

Rotten Floorboards in *Winter Splinter*. Online. Corpus Christi, TX. December 24, 2024.

Tantalize in *SEX/X/Y ZINE*. Norman, AR. May 2025.

Thank You in *Boundless Anthology*. McAllen, TX. April 2024.

The Ride Home in *Voices de la Luna: A Quarterly Literature & Arts Magazine*. Online. San Antonio, TX August 2023.

Where does love go in *Texas Bards*. October 2024.

Many texts were consulted and some quoted:

    Grateful Dead Fire on the Mountain.

    Bob Kaufman, The Ancient Rain.

    Jack Kerouac, On The Road.

    James Douglas Morrison, An American Prayer.

    Carol Coffee Reposa, Sailing West.

    Stendhal, The Red and The Black.

    Hunter S. Thompson, Hells Angles.

    Leo Tolstoy, Anna Karenina.

About the Author

Tom Murphy is the 2021-2022 Corpus Christi Poet Laureate and the Langdon Review's 2022 Writer-In-Residence. Murphy's books include When I Wear Bob Kaufman's Eyes (2022), Snake Woman Moon (2021), Pearl (2020), American History (2017), and co-edited with Alan Berecka Stone Renga (2017). His web page is http://tom-murphywriter.com

www.ingramcontent.com/pod-product-compliance
Lightning Source LLC
Chambersburg PA
CBHW022112090426
42743CB00008B/815